A Study Guide for

7 SECRETS
of the
EUCHARIST

by Vinny Flynn

A Study Guide for

7 SECRETS
of the
EUCHARIST

by Vinny Flynn

ENCOUNTERING
THE HEART OF GOD

Mary Flynn

MercySong IGNATIUS

PUBLISHED BY MERCYSONG, INC.
Stockbridge, Massachusetts USA
www.mercysong.com

IN COLLABORATION WITH IGNATIUS PRESS
Exclusive Distributor
San Francisco, California, USA

Library of Congress Control No. 2009939046

ISBN: 978-1-884479-42-7

Cover design by Riz Boncan Marsella

PRINTED IN THE UNITED STATES OF AMERICA
March 2010

"I came that they may have life
and have it abundantly."

Jn 10:10

CONTENTS

FOREWORD
An Invitation to Intimacy

"I slept but my heart was awake.
Listen! My lover is knocking ..."
Song of Solomon 5:2 NIV

When my father's book, *7 Secrets of the Eucharist,* was first released, I remember reading it for the first time and thinking how clever it was that each chapter wasn't just a chapter, but a "secret." Think about secrets. When someone tells you a secret, isn't it exciting? Don't you just want to know everything about it?

Now think about mysteries. Mysteries are similar to secrets, in that they intrigue us and beg to be examined, explored, pondered, and eventually, solved. We're dealing with the mysteries of God here, which we will never fully solve in this life. And these "secrets" of the Eucharist are more exciting than any other secrets imaginable; they are all part of a deeper mystery just waiting to be delved into, a mystery that could change your life ... the mystery of the Eucharist.

Life Changing?

You might be wondering how studying a sacrament could change your life. Let me put it to you this way. Have you ever longed to find deeper meaning in your life? To wake up one day and discover that there's something more to living than merely surviving? Do you wish you could be grateful every day just to be alive, no matter what comes your way?

The Eucharist offers each of us an incredible invitation: to become intimately one with God Himself, in a personal, one-on-one relationship. If you are willing to accept this invitation, the Eucharist can be that deeper meaning in your life, that something more, that one reason to get out of bed each day.

Awareness

It is my ultimate hope that through this study guide you will come to a deeper awareness of just how great a gift the Eucharist is. I am convinced that the more your awareness and knowledge grow, the more you will come to know and long for the great love that awaits you in the Eucharist.

"Listen!"

The Eucharist is a personal invitation from God's Heart to yours. God is calling to you as to the beloved in the Song of Solomon. He is beckoning you to enter into His Heart, and asking for permission to enter into yours. He will not force

Himself upon you, but He will *never* stop pursuing you.

"I slept but my heart was awake." Like the beloved, are you awake and listening for the Lord in your heart of hearts? Through the Eucharist, He is inviting you into a relationship that could become the most important thing in your entire life. "Listen!" The great Lover of your soul is knocking on the door of your heart ... will you accept His invitation to intimacy?

How to Use This Study Guide

There is no right or wrong way to use a study guide. You may decide to go through it on your own, get together and discuss the material with a few friends, or maybe even form a larger study group at your church. Each person has his or her own way of learning and processing information, so my advice would be to pray about it and pick the way you think will benefit you most.

There are a few things that are important to do regardless of which way you choose to use this study guide. The number one thing is *prayer*. Whether you are alone, with a few friends, or in a large group, *always* begin and end the study session with prayer. It doesn't have to be a lengthy supplication, but it shouldn't be rushed either, as if it's just something to get over with so you can get to the "important part" of the session. When you pray, make it a heartfelt, yet simple prayer directly to God. Thank Him for allowing you this time to study about this great Sacrament, and ask Him to bless your efforts and give you grace to enlighten your mind. Talk to the Lord as to a friend, but also remember to make praise and thanksgiving a part of every prayer:

✞ Thank You, Lord, for Your presence in the Most Holy Eucharist!

✞ I thank You for giving me this chance to learn more about You.

✞ I ask You to bless this time and to fill me with Your Holy Spirit so that I may be brought to a new level of understanding, a new level of faith, and a new level of love for You.

At the end of each session you can say a similar prayer in thanksgiving for whatever you learned and/or discussed. You can also relate it specifically to the secret just studied. Again, it doesn't have to be long or involve big words; just let it be sincere and unaffected:

✞ Jesus, I praise you for this time ... I thank You for guiding me through this secret, and for bringing me closer to You in the Eucharist. Continue to lead me, and draw me ever deeper into Your presence.

If you wish, you may use these prayers for every secret, or you may want to make up your own. I would encourage you to be as spontaneous as possible when you pray, because making up your own prayers is a great way to become more comfortable talking to the Lord in a personal way.

The second important thing to remember when going through a study guide is to make sure you set aside enough time for prayer and discussion or journaling. This is essential in a group, but it's good to keep in mind even when studying alone (other than the discussion, of course, unless you enjoy talking to yourself!).

Lastly, don't be afraid to make it personal. In this particular study guide most of the questions are written in a way that is meant to challenge you to go deeper. I encourage you to take these questions seriously, and really think about how these beautiful truths are affecting you personally. If you are in a group, you may choose to share some of these inward thoughts, or you can keep reflecting on them in your own heart. The questions are designed to be thought provoking, so take your time with them, and dig deep.

For Group Leaders

As a group leader, you should make it a priority to read ahead in the study guide, and really prepare for each session. You will be expected to know the material better than anyone else in the group, and the members will look to you for answers, guidance, prayer support, and encouragement. If you are meeting once a week, that will give you plenty of time to go through the material in a spirit of prayer, and let each secret sit with you and work in your heart. Remember to pray for the members of your group, that they will be open to whatever the Lord wants to reveal to them.

You will be responsible for leading the group in prayer, and leading them through each session as well. Others in your group may be comfortable with leading prayer, so you may decide to ask for volunteers at times. I wouldn't recommend, however, that you entirely forfeit your leadership in this area.

A group leader is also the timekeeper. Try to show up early for each session, and always begin and end on time. Bring enthusiasm and energy to every discussion, and affirm those who share personal thoughts with the group. Try to stay on topic, and avoid digressions as much as possible. In almost every group there will be a "Chatty Cathy" or "Jabbering Joe," who tends to monopolize the conversation. You may need to step in and make sure there is time for others to share their thoughts.

But be careful, because it can also be easy for a leader to talk too much, especially if the group members don't have a lot to say at first. Try to be aware of just how much time you spend talking. Ask a lot of questions, listen to what each person has to say, and guide the overall direction of the conversation. Being in a leadership position is a great responsibility; remember that your job is merely to be an instrument for God. "He must increase but I must decrease" (John 3:30). In any role such as this, you must die to yourself and let Christ shine through you, so that those with whom you come in contact will see the Lord in all your words and actions.

Finally, I would just like to say welcome aboard! Working on this project has been a great joy for me, and has brought me to a much deeper awareness and appreciation of the Lord's presence in the Blessed Sacrament. I hope you enjoy going through *7 Secrets of the Eucharist* with me, and I will be praying for you as you take this next step toward getting to know Jesus in the Eucharist.

$\mathscr{S}$ECRET 1
The Eucharist is alive

Reflection

R e-read the section on pages 9-11 when the Angel of Peace, in his third visit to the children, taught them the Fatima prayer, and showed them how to adore the Lord in the Eucharist. What was young Francisco's response to this experience?

_____

_____

_____

_____

_____

The author uses this scene to present us with an invitation: "We can treat God as a dead object, or we can prostrate our whole beings in front of Him." What are some practical ways to re-focus your mind and heart on adoring Jesus in the Eucharist throughout your day?

_____

_____

_____

_____

_____

Discussion or Journaling

❶ When at Mass, what distracts you from focusing on our Lord in the Eucharist? What can you do to help eliminate these distractions?

_____

_____

_____

_____

_____

❷ When you receive the Eucharist, do the words, "The Body of Christ" bring to mind the dead body of Christ on the Cross, or the living and glorious Christ? Why is it important to make this distinction?

_____

_____

_____

_____

_____

❸ In every reception of Holy Communion, this living and glorious Christ desires to become one with you in a profoundly personal way. What is the difference between believing this truth with your mind rather than your heart? Why is it sometimes easier to believe this truth with your mind?

_____

_____

_____

_____

_____

④ Christ desires to make you more fully alive through the Eucharist. What do you think it means to be "more fully alive"? How can you make this a reality in your everyday life?

_____

_____

_____

_____

Challenge Yourself

Next time you plan to attend Mass and receive Jesus in Holy Communion, prepare well. Dress appropriately — this is the Wedding Feast of the Lamb. Even if your schedule is tight, try to arrive early and take some time for prayer before Mass.

When you receive the Eucharist, be mindful of Who you are receiving, and prostrate yourself *interiorly* in adoration before the Living God. Open your whole being to His life-giving love, and think about the significance of your heart becoming one with His. After Mass, linger with the Lord, praising Him and thanking Him for His presence within you.

Going Deeper
(Readings found on pg. 61)

Scripture: Jn 6:33-35; Jn 6:47-51
Catechism: 1387; 1391
Diary of St. Faustina: 1324; 1447

Musings ...

As I was re-reading this first chapter, what really jumped out at me was the invitation on page 11: "We can treat God as a dead object, or we can prostrate our whole beings in front of Him, in *adoration,* in *gratitude,* in *love,* in *reparation.*" We are each called to console the Heart of God, not only as Church, but also as individuals. If you adore Christ in the Eucharist with this intent, you are not only consoling His Heart, but also demonstrating your love for Him.

In the same way, when you praise and thank Him, you are making reparation for all those souls who are indifferent to Him. By putting your energy toward worshipping God and praising Him for His goodness, you will find it much easier to focus on His blessings and less on your troubles. I challenge you to make praise and gratitude central to your daily life — you will be surprised at the difference it makes.

"O give thanks to the Lord, call on his name,
make known his deeds among the peoples!
Sing to him, sing praises to him,
tell of all his wonderful works!
Glory in his holy name; let the hearts of
those who seek the Lord rejoice!"

1 Chronicles 16:8-10

Notes

SECRET 2
Christ is not alone

Reflection

Even though only Jesus is sacramentally present in the Eucharist, the "whole celestial court," including the Father and the Spirit, is present with Him. Look again at the section on the Incarnation, found on pages 21-22. How can this teaching help you better understand the idea that Christ is not alone?

_____

_____

_____

_____

The author mentions several saints who experienced incredible intimacy with the Lord at Holy Communion. These saints recognized that the Holy Trinity dwelt within them, and they tried to respond to this great love more and more. At every reception of the Eucharist your body, too, becomes a dwelling for the Trinity. How does this knowledge affect how you will treat your body? How does it affect how you will treat others?

_____

_____

_____

_____

_____

Discussion or Journaling

❶ Christ does not multiply or divide Himself to be present in all the tabernacles of the world. All the saints in heaven, and all who receive the Eucharist here on earth, are united with the same Christ. How does this knowledge make you more aware of the Church as the one Body of Christ? How does this console you when far away from loved ones, and challenge you in regard to those you don't get along with very well?

_____

_____

_____

_____

❷ What is the significance of being united not only with the body and blood of Christ, but also His soul and divinity? How can this union help you remain focused on the ultimate union of eternity, even amidst the distractions of daily life?

_____

_____

_____

_____

❸ In every reception of the Eucharist, the Holy Trinity enters your being and dwells in your soul. What can you do to make yourself a better dwelling for the Most High God?

_____

_____

_____

_____

❹ God's love for you is so passionate that He desires to come to you in the intimacy of the Eucharist and *live* in you. Is this hard for you to believe? If so, why?

_____

_____

_____

_____

Challenge Yourself

Next time you go to Mass, make a point to thank the Lord for His love for you. Thank Him for His great willingness and desire to come to you in Holy Communion. Ask Him to help you understand the beautiful Eucharistic mystery of the indwelling of the Trinity. Take it a step further, and ask Him to show you how to love Him more, and to give you the grace to respond to Him more fully, that He may live in you in a new and deeper way.

> ### *Going Deeper*
> (Readings found on pg. 63)
>
> *Scripture:* Lk 17:21; Jn 14:23; Ez 37:27
> *Catechism:* 1377; 259; 260
> *Diary of St. Faustina:* 734; 911

Musings ...

Wow, what a gift! Not only does Jesus want to have a personal relationship with each of us, but the Father and the Holy Spirit do as well! We are so blessed to have such a personal God, Who gives Himself totally to us in this intimate way. What can we do to more fully enter into this awesome mystery? What prayers can we say, what praises can we sing, to really communicate our gratitude?

If you can, spend a little extra time in front of the Blessed Sacrament, gazing upon our humble Lord and praising Him for His goodness. It is in this way, through praise and thanksgiving, that you and I can show our love to the immense Heart of God, and grow in our appreciation for the beautiful gift that He has given us.

*"Enter his gates with thanksgiving
and his courts with praise;
give thanks to him and praise his name."*

Psalm 100:4 (NIV)

Notes

_____

_____

_____

_____

_____

_____

_____

_____

_____

_____

_____

_____

_____

_____

_____

_____

_____

_____

_____

_____

_____

_____

_____

_____

_____

_____

_____

$\mathcal{S}$ECRET 3

There is only one Mass

Reflection

Beginning on the bottom of page 41, review the Paschal Mystery section, continuing on until the end of the second paragraph on page 43. At every Mass, the Paschal Mystery is made present to us in our time and place. This means that at each Mass the veil of Heaven is lifted, and we are brought into the Holy of Holies.

Knowing this, what changes can you make to better prepare yourself before Mass? What can you do to more fully enter into this awesome experience?

_____

_____

_____

_____

_____

Because of his close sacramental identification with Jesus, each priest celebrates the Mass *in persona Christi*, which means he acts *in the person of Christ*. In spite of this amazing reality, priests are not perfect, and sometimes it's easy to judge them when they do not meet all our expectations. Keeping in mind their close connection with Christ, what are some things you can focus on to help you be more grateful for the priests who serve you?

_____

_____

_____

_____

_____

Discussion or Journaling

1 In an effort to find meaning in the Mass, many people "shop around" until they find a Mass that best suits them. What do you look for in a Mass? Has reading this chapter changed how you view the Mass?

_____

_____

_____

_____

_____

2 Each Mass is "a foretaste" of the eternal liturgy that is constantly taking place in heaven, and we join with all of heaven and earth in celebrating this liturgy. How can seeing this bigger picture of the Mass help you to more fully enter into the Mass?

_____

_____

_____

_____

_____

❸ The Mass is our participation in the one eternal liturgy. What are some things that might cause you to lose sight of this amazing reality? What can help you see this more clearly?

_____

_____

_____

_____

_____

❹ The priest is the "steward of the mysteries of God," and it is his responsibility and privilege to bring us the Eucharist. Why is this such a privilege for the priest, and why is it so important that he not change or modify the liturgy?

_____

_____

_____

_____

_____

Challenge Yourself

When you go to Mass, sit quietly beforehand, and think about the one eternal liturgy that is going on in heaven all the time. *This* is the liturgy you are about to participate in.

When Mass begins, if the music is not to your liking, don't judge the musicians; think instead about their willingness to join the choir of angels in praising the Lord. If the priest gives a less than satisfactory homily, or does things differently than you're used to, refuse to give in to negativity and criticism — even if that negativity is only in your head. Instead, make a conscious decision to recognize and respect his sacramental identification with Christ, and strive to see him in the light of the heavenly liturgy.

Most of all, thank God for the gift of the priesthood, without which, we would not have the Mass, nor the joy of the Eucharist.

> ### *Going Deeper*
> **(Readings found on pg. 66)**
>
> *Scripture:* Heb 7:27; Heb 10:10; Rom 6:10
> *Catechism:* 1085; 1370; 1410
> *Diary of St. Faustina:* 953; 1052

Musings ...

Once I was able to get past all the theology in this chapter, I found myself overcome with gratitude for the Sacrament of Holy Orders. I know I'm supposed to be talking about the Eucharist, but if you'll remember, this book does quote Pope John Paul II, who says, "there can be no Eucharist without the priesthood, just as there can be no priesthood without the Eucharist." How beautiful is this gift that is given the priest, and through the priest, to us!

Lately I have been more and more convicted of how much our priests do for us, and that we must constantly support and surround them in prayer, along with our seminarians and future priests. Some priests may not be who we think they ought to be, or who we need them to be. Some may even wound us, but that is all the more reason why they need our prayers.

So many blessings come to us through our beloved priests, and so I encourage you to affirm, support, and pray for your priests, all the while praising and thanking God for His gifts of the priesthood and the Eucharist.

> "*Give thanks to the Lord, for he is good;*
> *his love endures forever.*"
> 1 Chronicles 16:34 (NIV)

Notes

_____

_____

_____

_____

_____

_____

_____

_____

_____

_____

_____

_____

_____

_____

_____

_____

_____

_____

_____

_____

_____

_____

$\mathscr{S}$ECRET 4

The Eucharist is not just one miracle

Reflection

Pope Leo XIII tells us that the Eucharist contains, through a "variety of miracles, all supernatural realities." Mull over the term "supernatural realities." What do you think that means?

Look over the review of the first three chapters, found on pages 57-58. Can you see how each one of these miracles is a supernatural reality? Which miracle stands out to you the most? Do any of these miracles help you grow in your awareness of what an amazing gift the Eucharist is?

_____

_____

_____

_____

_____

The Catechism says that the Eucharist is the "goal of all the sacraments." Look at each of the remaining six sacraments:

Baptism, Reconciliation, Confirmation, Holy Matrimony, Holy Orders, and the Anointing of the Sick. How does each of these sacraments bring us closer to our Lord in the Eucharist?

_____

_____

_____

_____

_____

_____

_____

Discussion or Journaling

❶ Many people have a hard time believing in miracles because they cannot be logically explained. Are you the kind of person who sometimes wants explanation or proof for things? If so, does this affect your belief in the Real Presence of Christ in the Eucharist?

_____

_____

_____

_____

_____

❷ The Eucharist is "a course of resplendent miracles," and thus should inspire awe and amazement; but it is very easy to lose sight of this in the distractions of daily life and to receive the Lord absentmindedly. What are some things that will help you retain this awe and receive the Lord with awareness and reverence?

_____

_____

_____

_____

_____

❸ The Eucharist contains "the Church's entire spiritual wealth" and "is the greatest treasure of the Church." How does this truth change how you feel about the Eucharist? Have you ever considered the Eucharist to be your greatest treasure?

_____

_____

_____

_____

_____

❹ Christ wants to accomplish miracles in us through the Eucharist and "fill us with every heavenly blessing and grace." What miracle do you need Christ to work in you? How can you be more open to being transformed by His presence in the Eucharist?

_____

_____

_____

Challenge Yourself

The next time you are able to go to Mass, think about the miracles that are about to take place. Bread and wine will be changed into the actual body, blood, soul, and divinity of Christ; Christ will be truly present, as He is in heaven — living and glorious — without leaving heaven; we will enter into the one eternal liturgy, and be in union with the entire created universe and *all* of heaven, including the Father and the Holy Spirit.

After Mass, spend more time than you usually would in thanksgiving. Give praise to God for His glory, and surrender yourself completely to Him that He might accomplish miracles in you through the Most Holy Eucharist.

> ### *Going Deeper*
> **(Readings found on pg. 68)**
>
> *Scripture:* Job 26:14; Rom 11:33
> *Catechism:* 1327; 1394; 1407
> *Diary of St. Faustina:* 914; 1392; 1670

Musings ...

At first glance, this chapter seemed to be only a summary of the past three chapters. But as I studied it, a phrase near the end caught my eye: "The Eucharist is 'the source and summit of the Christian life.'"

Whoa. Time-out. This is not just some vague theological statement; this is an intense, and rather daunting challenge. Look honestly at your life. Look long and hard, because this is more than just a little important.

Are you living solely for the Eucharist? Do you do the things you do out of love and devotion for the Eucharist? Is making time for worshipping Jesus in the Blessed Sacrament on the top of your daily priority list? Does the fact that God longs to intimately unite Himself with you in the Eucharist thrill you to the very core of your being? *Because this is our faith!* This is what it really means to be a Christian, to be a follower of Christ.

Why? Because this is how He chose to remain with us until the end of time. If you have ever wondered what our faith is all about, what is really underneath it all, then this is your answer.

I strongly urge you to re-commit your entire life to the Lord. Ask Him for the grace to undertake this great challenge, this new way of living. Above all, continue to praise Him, for it is in praise of God that we are made like Him. This can only bring us closer to living a life centered on the Eucharist.

"Hear O Israel!
The Lord is our God, the Lord alone!
Therefore, you shall love the Lord,
your God, with all your heart,
and with all your soul,
and with all your strength."
Deuteronomy 6:4-5 (NAB)

Notes

_____

_____

_____

_____

_____

_____

_____

_____

_____

_____

_____

_____

_____

_____

_____

_____

_____

_____

_____

_____

_____

_____

_____

_____

$\mathcal{S}$ECRET 5
We don't just receive

Reflection

Go back to pages 63-65 and find the "action" words that describe how we should respond to the invitation given us at each Holy Communion. Is it difficult for you to actively encounter Christ in the Eucharist? Receiving Holy Communion is not just about God dwelling within us; it involves relationship. Do you sometimes struggle with the idea of being in such an intimate relationship with God? If so, why?

_____

_____

_____

_____

_____

In order for us to respond to this invitation of Christ, the Catechism says "we must prepare ourselves for so great and so holy a moment." On pages 65-66 the author lists the *minimum* requirements given by the Church. Why do you think these requirements are so important? Do you avoid any of them? Can you think of any other ways to prepare yourself for Holy Communion?

_____

_____

_____

_____

_____

Discussion or Journaling

❶ The word "receive" can sometimes be misleading when speaking of our participation in Holy Communion. How is Our Lady's perfect response at the Annunciation and the Visitation a model for us? How can Mary help us prepare to fully receive our Lord?

_____

_____

_____

_____

_____

❷ Have you ever thought about the way you receive the Eucharist? When in line for Holy Communion, what goes through your mind? What do you reflect on once you return to your pew?

_____

_____

_____

_____

_____

❸ In Holy Communion we are called to intimately unite ourselves with Christ, and become one flesh with Him. How do you feel about using this nuptial imagery in reference to the Eucharist?

_____

_____

_____

_____

_____

❹ How much time do you usually take in preparation for Holy Communion? How much time do you spend in thanksgiving after receiving? Why is it so important to prepare and give thanks, and why is it so easy for other things to take on more importance?

_____

_____

_____

_____

_____

Challenge Yourself

Next time you walk down the aisle to receive Jesus in the

Eucharist, try not to think of Him as just some impersonal God, or even as only your Savior. Imagine Him as the Bridegroom of your soul, waiting for you with radiant expectation. (Whether you are a man or a woman, you are called to unite yourself in this type of intimate, nuptial relationship with Christ in the Eucharist). Ask Mary to prepare your heart to receive Him.

Ask the Lord for the desire to give yourself completely to Him in a union of love, that He might totally submerge you in the ocean of His mercy. Don't leave directly after Mass, but stay and remain lost in the moment with Jesus, thanking Him for His all-consuming love for you.

> ### *Going Deeper*
> **(Readings found on pg. 70)**
>
> *Scripture:* Jn 15:4-5; Lk 1:38
> *Catechism:* 1329; 1385; 1386
> *Diary of St. Faustina:* 1805-1806; 1721

Musings ...

For this secret, I decided to look up the literal meanings of the word "receive." The first meaning is to accept or obtain something. When we receive the Eucharist, we are indeed obtaining a great gift ... but it's so much more than that. The next meaning was what really jumped out at me: to welcome. Ah, there it is. This is how we must receive Christ, by welcoming Him into our hearts as we would a loved one.

At the end of this chapter I unearthed another gem. In a meditation on the Eucharist, St. Francis of Assisi told his brothers, "Hold back nothing of yourselves for yourselves, that He who gives Himself totally to you may receive you totally!" Our Lady gives us the perfect example of this at the Annunciation when she completely surrenders her entire being to God so that His will may be done.

The Lord desires to be one flesh with you, no holds barred. Delve deep into your heart. Are there any areas in your life that you have not yet given over to Him? When you receive the Eucharist, do you also desire to be fully one with the Lord, or are you using spiritual contraception? Are some chambers of your heart locked to even the Lover of your soul?

You are the cherished one of the Lord! Give Him everything: your sorrows, your joys, your insecurities, your desires, your anger, your bitterness, and your pain. He will purify all in the fire of His love.

"Behold, I stand at the door and knock ..."
Revelation 3:20

Notes

_____

_____

_____

_____

_____

_____

_____

_____

_____

_____

_____

_____

_____

_____

_____

_____

_____

_____

_____

_____

_____

_____

_____

_____

_____

_____

_____

$\mathscr{S}$ECRET 6
Every reception is different

Reflection

R e-read from the top of page 74 to the middle of page 76. The author reiterates St. Thomas' teaching that it is our spiritual disposition that determines what effect (if any) the Eucharist will have upon our souls. What are the potential dangers if your spiritual disposition is not what it ought to be? What are some ways you can make sure you are not a "false" person?

_____

_____

_____

_____

_____

At the very end of the chapter, the author contrasts the "bad news" with the "good news." Knowing that *what* we receive depends on *how* we receive shouldn't frighten us away from the Eucharist; it should make us excited that we have the freedom to make every reception better and more intimate than the last. Does receiving the Eucharist excite you? What will help you anticipate your next Holy Communion?

_____

_____

_____

_____

_____

Discussion or Journaling

1 If someone asked you to give one reason why receiving Holy Communion is so important to you, what reason would you give?

_____

_____

_____

_____

_____

2 It's very easy to receive the Eucharist routinely, especially if you are fatigued or distracted. Do you ever notice a difference between this kind of reception in contrast to when you make a concentrated effort to enter into each Holy Communion?

_____

_____

_____

_____

❸ St. Thomas Aquinas says that one is a "false" person if he or she does not desire union with Christ in the Eucharist and does not try to remove any obstacle to this union. Do you think it is difficult or easy to be a false person? Why?

_____

_____

_____

_____

_____

❹ Oftentimes, many people refrain from receiving Holy Communion out of fear, doubt, or over-scrupulosity. Have you ever found yourself in this position? What has kept you from receiving the Eucharist?

_____

_____

_____

_____

_____

Challenge Yourself

Resolve to make your next Mass a completely new experience. Examine your conscience and think about your spiritual disposition. Maybe go over some of the material discussed in some of the previous chapters, just to have it in your mind as you prepare.

Do not stop making preparation when Mass begins; continue to prepare your heart until the time you actually receive the Lord. Remember to ask Mary to help you in your preparation. You will never be able to prepare well enough for this incredible gift, so do not think that a few minutes before Mass is all that is necessary.

Use the time after Communion to sit in the stillness of your heart with the Lord, believing with faith that He has become one with you in a perfect union of love.

> ### *Going Deeper*
> **(Readings found on pg. 73)**
>
> *Scripture:* Jn 6:51, 54, 56; 1 Cor 6:17
> *Catechism:* 1389; 1418
> *Diary of St. Faustina:* 156; 717; 1289

Musings ...

Two things really spoke to me in this chapter, both from St. Augustine. As cited on page 78, "Let no one eat Christ's flesh before he first worships it." Wow. "Let *no one* eat Christ's flesh before he first worships it." This seems like pretty clear instruction to me; before we dine at the table of the Master, we must first worship Him. How do we worship Him? *Eucharistic Adoration*.

I pray that if anything stays with you, it will be the desire to adore our Lord in the Eucharist. Do you know that He waits for *you*? He anticipates *your* coming. This is mind blowing! Who is this God of ours?

On to the next piece of wisdom from St. Augustine: "This is our daily bread: take it daily that it may profit you daily." Hmmm, St. Augustine likes being straightforward, doesn't he? If the Eucharist really is all the Church teaches, if everything in this book is true, if the Lord really wants to unite Himself intimately with you in every Holy Communion, *will you not take advantage of this?*

If you want your life to be radically changed, go to Daily Mass and Eucharistic Adoration as often as possible. Make the Eucharist the center of your life, and discover what it means to live "through Him, with Him, and in Him."

> "*Give to the Lord the glory he deserves!*
> *Bring your offering and come into his presence.*
> *Worship the Lord in all his holy splendor.*"
> 1 Chronicles 16:29 (NLT)

Notes

_____

_____

_____

_____

_____

_____

_____

_____

_____

_____

_____

_____

_____

_____

_____

_____

_____

_____

_____

_____

_____

_____

_____

_____

_____

$\mathcal{S}$ECRET 7

There's no limit to the number of times we can receive

Reflection

$\mathcal{S}$t. Maximilian Kolbe explains, "At times, spiritual Communion brings the same graces as sacramental." Why then, is it still necessary for us to receive sacramentally? Go back to page 86 and find the answer to this question. Review pages 87-88. Why is it so important to receive spiritually as well as sacramentally? How can you make every spiritual Communion an anticipation of sacramental Communion?

_____

_____

_____

_____

_____

The author tells us that every moment can become an occasion for making a spiritual Communion. Both St. Maximilian Kolbe and St. Francis de Sales resolved to make a spiritual

Communion every fifteen minutes to help them remain focused on the Lord during the day.

How often do everyday things cause you to lose focus on God's presence in your soul? With this in mind, how many times a day do you think you need to make a spiritual Communion?

_____

_____

_____

_____

_____

Discussion or Journaling

❶ St. Thomas says there are two ways to receive the Eucharist, sacramental and spiritual. Which way do you think most people receive? Which way do you most often receive?

_____

_____

_____

_____

_____

❷ Spiritual Communion is commonly thought of as merely something you do when "real" Communion isn't available. How has this chapter changed the way you view spiritual Communion?

_____

_____

_____

_____

_____

❸ Many of the saints made spiritual Communion a daily oc-
currence, and even a way of life. How can you make spiritual
Communion an important part of your daily life?

_____

_____

_____

_____

_____

❹ Throughout our lives we each go through a continuing pro-
cess of spiritual growth. How can you see spiritual Communion helping you along your spiritual journey?

_____

_____

_____

_____

_____

Challenge Yourself

Now you no longer have to wait until your next Mass to
unite yourself with Jesus in the Eucharist. Every spare minute

you have, make a spiritual Communion and invite the Lord into your heart.

When you wake up in the morning, let it be the first thing you do, before you even get out of bed. During your daily tasks, take a step back, and refocus yourself on His presence within you.

At night, make a spiritual Communion before you fall asleep, the Name of Jesus being the last word on your lips. Never cease giving thanks to the Lord for His presence in the Eucharist, and for this beautiful way to unite yourself even more with Him.

> ### *Going Deeper*
> **(Readings found on pg. 75)**
>
> *Scripture:* Jn 15:9-11; Jer 29:13-14
> *Catechism:* 2565; 2014
> *Diary of St. Faustina:* 318; 1821; 1303

Musings ...

This chapter is, in a sense, the culmination of all the secrets presented in the book. Think about what every reception of the Eucharist offers: Christ, living and glorious, desires to become one with you, and *live* in you; you become a dwelling place for the Most Holy Trinity and the whole celestial court; you are lifted out of time and into Heaven where you participate in the one eternal liturgy; you are invited to unite yourself intimately in relationship with your Creator and Lord; and you are given the opportunity to make every reception better than the last.

Spiritual Communion is how we can enter into this mystery *at any moment*. Remember that phrase, "The Eucharist is the source and summit of the Christian life"? It is through spiritual Communion that this goal can be reached. The more you receive spiritually, the more you will anticipate receiving sacramentally. The more eager you are to receive sacramentally, the more you will be made aware of the great love that God longs to bestow on you through the Eucharist.

This growing awareness will only increase your love for the Lord, and instill in you a desire to praise Him as you have never praised before.

> "*Come, let us bow down in worship,*
> *let us kneel before the Lord our Maker...*"
> Psalm 96:6 (NIV)

Notes

AFTERWORD
Welcome to Life

"This is eternal life: that they may know you,
the only true God, and Jesus Christ,
whom you have sent."
John 17:3 (NIV)

As you come to the end of this study on the Eucharist, I pray that it has been a profoundly personal journey for you, one that you wish to venture deeper and deeper into. If you have been at all touched by anything you learned here, or if anything you discovered has brought you closer to the Heart of God, this could be the beginning of a brand-new way of life for you: the eternal life that flows from the Eucharist.

You might be wondering where to go from here. Maybe you were familiar with some of the material covered in *7 Secrets of the Eucharist*, or maybe most of it was new to you. Either way, you might not be sure what do with all of this information swimming around in your head! It can be a little overwhelming, but don't worry; there are a few simple ways to put everything you have learned into practice.

Make it personal

While writing this study guide, I noticed a theme emerging. This theme eventually became the central focus of my writing: *Encountering the Heart of God.* I love the intimate meaning that the word "encounter" takes on here, because it is a reminder that the Lord is continually calling you to His Heart in the Eucharist.

How can you enter into this heart-to-Heart? By giving praise and thanksgiving to the Lord. *How* you praise Him isn't important; how *often* you praise Him is what matters. Whether it be through song or dance, in words or tongues, or simply with a quiet gratitude felt in your heart, your praise will unite your heart with His, strengthening the bond of love created by the Eucharist.

Praise may be difficult at first because it requires a complete self-abandonment. But the more you consciously try to forget yourself in praise of God, the more natural it becomes.

In 1 Thessalonians 5:18, St. Paul tells us to "give thanks in all circumstances." Pray for the desire and grace to follow this advice in your everyday life. Never stop going deeper! Start small by simply thanking the Lord every day for the gift of His presence in the Blessed Sacrament, and praising Him for His great love for you.

The more you praise, especially in Eucharistic Adoration, the more your life will become centered on the Eucharist. The Eucharist is supposed to be "the source and summit" of your whole life, remember? In order for you to really make this goal

---

a reality, all must be surrendered to the Lord. All doors must be opened to Him, even those doors that you would rather keep closed.

Follow the example of Mary at the Annunciation and give all of yourself to God for Him to do with as He pleases. In this act of complete trust and faith, you are abandoning yourself totally to the Lord, so that your heart will be one with His.

Build relationship

Three concrete ways to deepen your awareness and appreciation of the Eucharist are daily Mass, spiritual Communion, and Eucharistic Adoration. If you are truly trying to make the Eucharist the source and summit of your life, daily Mass will be important to you. You can stay focused on the Lord's presence within you through spiritual Communion, even if it's been hours since you received sacramentally.

Adoration can take place wherever the Eucharist is present and will help your spiritual growth immensely. Many churches even have perpetual Adoration chapels, making it easy for the faithful to stop by at any hour of the day or night.

Think about it in a more personal way. When you are getting to know someone, don't you want to spend time with that person? And if you really fall in love with that person, wouldn't you want to be in touch every day, not just once, but throughout the day? Essentially, this is the purpose of these three things: to draw you deeper into that personal, one-on-one relationship with God.

Pass it on

Remember at the beginning of the book when I talked about how exciting it is when someone tells you a secret? What happens when it's a really good secret? Isn't it hard not to tell anyone? Don't you just want to shout it from the rooftops?

Well, I've got something to tell you. Are you ready? As my father explained in *7 Secrets of the Eucharist*, these "secrets" aren't actually secrets, but many people don't know about them. And the great thing is that not only are we *allowed* to tell others, we're *supposed* to! "Go out to all the world and tell the good news" (Mark 16:15).

We can spread the good news by word of mouth, but even more importantly, through our actions. When we receive the Eucharist we, like Mary, are supposed to go "in haste" and bring the Lord to others in visitations of our own.

That's what the dismissal at Mass really means: "Let us *go forth.*" Not just "go forth" (as in leave the church building), but go forth as Mary did, bringing Christ to the world.

That's a pretty tall order. How do *we* bring Christ to the world? *We become living Eucharist.* Think about that. Every time you receive the Lord in the Blessed Sacrament you become one flesh with Him and He lives in you. When you then leave the church and go about your daily life, if you stay continually aware of His presence within you through spiritual Communion, your entire life will be a reflection of God's presence to those around you. You will go forth as a monstrance, radiating the light of Christ to the world.

If you'll remember, Mary didn't have to say much when she reached her cousin's house; Elizabeth was completely filled with the Holy Spirit at the sound of Mary's greeting! Mary was so transparent to God that His light enveloped Elizabeth and made John the Baptist leap for joy within the womb of his mother.

Mary is our model, and we must strive, with her intercession, to reach her level of transparency so that the Lord can work through our weakness to touch the lives of others.

So pass it on! Continue your search for a deeper relationship with the Lord, the Great Lover of your soul. Praise Him and thank Him for his love and mercy. Make time to adore Him in the Blessed Sacrament; spend precious hours getting to know Him and just sitting in His presence. Live for your next spiritual Communion, and live in anticipation of your next sacramental Communion. Become living Eucharist and carry Christ to others, following Our Lady's example of complete self-donation. Ask her to help you make every moment an encounter with the Heart of God. Embrace this new way of living that the Eucharist offers, this eternal life that comes from knowing the only true God.

"Eternal life must begin already here on earth through Holy Communion"
Diary of St. Faustina, 1811

Notes

GOING DEEPER

SECRET 1

Scripture

"'For the bread of God is that which comes down from heaven, and gives life to the world.' They said to him, 'Lord, give us this bread always.' Jesus said to them, 'I am the bread of life; he who comes to me shall not hunger, and he who believes in me shall never thirst.'"

— John 6:33-35

"'Truly, truly, I say to you, he who believes has eternal life. I am the bread of life. Your fathers ate the manna in the wilderness, and they died. This is the bread which comes down from heaven, that a man may eat of it and not die. I am the living bread which came down from heaven; if any one eats of this bread, he will live forever; and the bread which I shall give for the life of the world is my flesh.'"

— John 6:47-51

Catechism

"To prepare for worthy reception of this sacrament, the faithful should observe the fast required in their Church. Bodily demeanor (gestures, clothing) ought to convey the respect, solemnity, and joy of this moment when Christ becomes our guest."

— CCC, 1387

"Holy Communion augments our union with Christ. The principal fruit of receiving the Eucharist in Holy Communion is an intimate union with Christ Jesus. Indeed, the Lord said: 'He who eats my flesh and drinks my blood abides in me, and I in him.' Life in Christ has its foundation in the Eucharistic banquet: 'As the living Father sent me, and I live because of the Father, so he who eats me will live because of me.'"

— CCC, 1391

Diary of St. Faustina

"I bow down before You, O Bread of Angels,
With deep faith, hope and love
And from the depths of my soul I worship You,
Though I am but nothingness.

"I bow down before You, O hidden God
And love you with all my heart.

The veils of mystery hinder me not at all;
I love You as do Your chosen ones in heaven.

"I bow down before You, O Lamb of God
Who take away the sins of my soul,
Whom I receive into my heart each morn,
You who are my saving help."

— Diary, 1324

"Oh, how painful it is to Me that souls so seldom unite them-
selves to Me in Holy Communion ... In order that you may
know at least some of My pain, imagine the most tender of
mothers who has great love for her children, while those children spurn her love. Consider her pain. No one is in a position to console her. This is but a feeble image and likeness of
My love."

— Diary, 1447

SECRET 2

Scripture

"The Kingdom of God is within you."

— Luke 17:21 (NIV)

"If a man loves me, he will keep my word, and my Father will love him, and we will come to him and make our dwelling with him."

— John 14:23

"My dwelling place will be with them; I will be their God, and they will be my people."

— Ezekiel 37:27 (NIV)

Catechism

"The Eucharistic presence of Christ begins at the moment of the consecration and endures as long as the Eucharistic species subsist. Christ is present whole and entire in each of the species and whole and entire in each of their parts, in such a way that the breaking of the bread does not divide Christ."

— CCC, 1377

"The whole Christian life is a communion with each of the divine persons, without in any way separating them."

— CCC, 259

"We are called to be a dwelling for the Most Holy Trinity."

— CCC, 260

Diary of St. Faustina

"I see that Jesus himself is acting in my soul during this retreat. And as for me, I try only to be faithful to His grace. I have submitted my soul completely to the influence of God. This Mighty Ruler of Heaven has taken entire possession of my soul. I feel that I am being lifted up above earth and heaven into the inner life of God, where I come to know the Father, the Son and the Holy Spirit, but always in the unity of majesty."

— Diary, 734

"On one occasion, God's presence pervaded my whole being, and my mind was mysteriously enlightened in respect to His Essence. He allowed me to understand His interior life. In spirit, I saw the Three Divine Persons, but Their Essence was One. He is One, and One only, but in Three Persons; none of Them is either greater or smaller; there is no difference in either beauty or sanctity, for They are One. They are absolutely One. His Love transported me into this knowledge and united me with Himself. When I was united to One, I was equally united to the Second and to the Third in such a way that when we are united with One, by that very fact, we are equally united to the two Persons in the same way as with the One. Their will is One, one God, though in Three Persons. When One of the Three Persons communicates with a soul, by the power of that one will, it finds itself united with the Three Persons and is inundated in the happiness flowing from the Most Holy Trinity, the same happiness that nourishes the saints."

— Diary, 911

SECRET 3

Scripture

"He has no need … to offer sacrifices daily, first for his own sins and then for those of the people; he did this once for all when he offered up himself."

— Hebrews 7:27

"We have been made holy through the sacrifice of the body of Jesus Christ once for all."

— Hebrews 10:10 (NIV)

"The death he died, he died to sin once for all."

— Romans 6:10

Catechism

"In the liturgy of the Church, it is principally his own Paschal mystery that Christ signifies and makes present. During his earthly life Jesus announced his Paschal mystery by his teaching and anticipated it by his actions. When his Hour comes, he lives out the unique event of history which does not pass away: Jesus dies, is buried, rises from the dead, and is seated at the right hand of the Father "once for all." His Paschal mystery is a real event that occurred in our history, but it is unique: all other historical events happen once, and then they pass away, swallowed up in the past. The Paschal mystery of

Christ, by contrast, cannot remain only in the past, because by his death he destroyed death, and all that Christ is — all that he did and suffered for all men — participates in the divine eternity, and so transcends all times while being made present in them all. The event of the Cross and Resurrection abides and draws everything toward life."

— CCC, 1085

"To the offering of Christ are united not only the members still here on earth, but also those already in the glory of heaven. In communion with and commemorating the Blessed Virgin Mary and all the saints, the Church offers the Eucharistic sacrifice. In the Eucharist the Church is as it were at the foot of the cross with Mary, united with the offering and intercession of Christ."

— CCC, 1370

"It is Christ himself, the eternal high priest of the New Covenant who, acting through the ministry of the priests, offers the Eucharistic sacrifice. And it is the same Christ, really present under the species of bread and wine, who is the offering of the Eucharistic sacrifice."

— CCC, 1410

Diary of St. Faustina

"I am suffering as much as my weak nature can bear... to beg for strength for priests. Oh, how much reverence I have for priests; and I am asking Jesus, the High Priest, to grant them many graces."

— Diary, 953

"O my Jesus, I beg You on behalf of the whole Church: grant it love and the light of Your Spirit, and give power to the words of priests so that hardened hearts might be brought to repentance and return to You, O Lord. Lord, give us holy priests; You yourself maintain them in holiness. O Divine and Great High Priest, may the power of Your mercy accompany them everywhere and protect them from the devil's traps and snares which are continually being set for the souls of priests. May the power of Your mercy, O Lord, shatter and bring to naught all that might tarnish the sanctity of priests, for You can do all things."

— Diary, 1052

SECRET 4

Scripture

"And these are but the outer fringe of his works; how faint the whisper we hear of him! Who then can understand the thunder of his power?"

— Job 26:14 (NIV)

"O the depth of the riches and wisdom and knowledge of God! How unsearchable are his judgments and how inscrutable his ways!"

— Romans 11:33

Catechism

"In brief, the Eucharist is the sum and summary of our faith: 'Our way of thinking is attuned to the Eucharist, and the Eucharist in turn confirms our way of thinking.'"

— CCC, 1327

"Since Christ died for us out of love, when we celebrate the memorial of his death at the moment of sacrifice we ask that love may be granted to us by the coming of the Holy Spirit. We humbly pray that in the strength of this love by which Christ willed to die for us, we, by receiving the gift of the Holy Spirit, may be able to consider the world as crucified for us, and to be ourselves as crucified to the world. ... Having received the gift of love, let us die to sin and live for God."

— CCC, 1394

"The Eucharist is the heart and the summit of the Church's life, for in it Christ associates his Church and all her members with his sacrifice of praise and thanksgiving offered once for all on the cross to his Father; by this sacrifice he pours out the graces of salvation on his Body which is the Church."

— CCC, 1407

Diary of St. Faustina

"A great mystery is accomplished in the Holy Mass. With what great devotion should we listen to and take part in this death of Jesus."

— Diary, 914

"All the good that is in me is due to Holy Communion. I owe everything to it. I feel that this holy fire has transformed me completely. Oh, how happy I am to be a dwelling place for You, O Lord! My heart is a temple in which You dwell continually."

— Diary, 1392

"During Mass, I thanked the Lord Jesus for having deigned to redeem us and for having given us that greatest of all gifts; namely, His love in Holy Communion; that is, His very own Self. At that moment, I was drawn into the bosom of the Most Holy Trinity, and I was immersed in the love of the Father, the Son and the Holy Spirit. These moments are hard to describe."

— Diary, 1670

SECRET 5

Scripture

"Abide in me as I abide in you. ... Those who abide in me and

I in them bear much fruit, because apart from me you can do nothing."

— Jn 15: 4-5

"Mary said, Behold, I am the handmaid of the Lord. May it be done to me according to your word."

— Luke 1:38 (NAB)

Catechism

"[The Eucharist is called] The Lord's Supper, because of its connection with the supper which the Lord took with his disciples on the eve of his Passion and because it anticipates the wedding feast of the Lamb in the heavenly Jerusalem."

— CCC, 1329

"To respond to this invitation we must prepare ourselves for so great and so holy a moment. St. Paul urges us to examine our conscience: 'Whoever, therefore, eats the bread or drinks the cup of the Lord in an unworthy manner will be guilty of profaning the body and blood of the Lord. Let a man examine himself, and so eat of the bread and drink of the cup. For any one who eats and drinks without discerning the body eats and drinks judgment upon himself.' Anyone conscious of a grave sin must receive the sacrament of Reconciliation before coming to communion."

— CCC, 1385

"Before so great a sacrament, the faithful can only echo humbly and with ardent faith the words of the Centurion: 'Domine, non sum dignus ut intres sub tectum meum, sed tantum dic verbo, et sanabitur anima mea' ('Lord, I am not worthy that you should enter under my roof, but only say the word and my soul will be healed')."

— CCC, 1386

Diary of St. Faustina

"Today, I am preparing myself for Your coming as a bride does for the coming of her bridegroom. He is a great Lord, this Bridegroom of mine. The heavens cannot contain Him. The seraphim who stand closest to Him cover their faces and repeat unceasingly: Holy, Holy, Holy. This great Lord is my Bridegroom. It is to Him that Choirs sing. It is before Him that the Thrones bow down. By His splendor the sun is eclipsed. And yet this great Lord is my Bridegroom. My heart, desist from this profound meditation on how others adore Him, for you no longer have time for that, as He is coming and is already at your door."

— Diary, 1805

"I go out to meet Him and I invite Him to the dwelling place of my heart, humbling myself profoundly before His majesty. But the Lord lifts me up from the dust and invites me, as his bride, to sit next to Him and to tell Him everything that is on my heart. And I, set at ease by His kindness, lean my head on

His breast and tell Him of everything."

— Diary, 1806

"After Holy Communion, when I had welcomed Jesus into my heart, I said to Him, 'My Love, reign in the most secret recesses of my heart, there where my most secret thoughts are conceived, where You alone have free access, in this deepest sanctuary where human thought cannot penetrate. May You alone dwell there, and may everything I do exteriorly take its origin in You. I ardently desire, and I am striving with all the strength of my soul, to make You, Lord feel at home in this sanctuary.'"

— Diary, 1721

SECRET 6

Scripture

"I am the living bread that came down from heaven; if any one eats of this bread, he will live for ever; ... he who eats my flesh and drinks my blood has eternal life and ... abides in me, and I in him."

— Jn 6:51, 54, 56

"He who unites himself with the Lord is one with him in spirit."

— 1 Cor. 6:17 (NIV)

Catechism

"The Church strongly encourages the faithful to receive the holy Eucharist on Sundays and feast days, or more often still, even daily."

— CCC, 1389

"Because Christ himself is present in the sacrament of the altar, he is to be honored with the worship of adoration. 'To visit the Blessed Sacrament is ... a proof of gratitude, an expression of love, and a duty of adoration toward Christ our Lord' (Paul VI, MF 66)."

— CCC, 1418

Diary of St. Faustina

"Once, I desired very much to receive Holy Communion, but I had a certain doubt, and I did not go. I suffered greatly because of this. It seemed to me that my heart would burst from the pain. When I set about my work, my heart full of bitterness, Jesus suddenly stood by me and said, My daughter, do not omit Holy Communion unless you know well that your fall was serious; apart from this, no doubt must stop you from uniting yourself with Me in the mystery of My love. Your minor faults will disappear in My love like a piece of straw thrown into a great furnace. Know that you grieve Me much when you fail to receive Me in Holy Communion."

— Diary, 156

"All night long, I was preparing to receive Holy Communion.
… My soul was flooded with love and repentance."

— Diary, 717

"Most sweet Jesus, set on fire my love for You and transform
me into Yourself. Divinize me that my deeds may be pleasing
to You. May this be accomplished by the power of the Holy
Communion which I receive daily. Oh, how greatly I desire to
be wholly transformed into You, O Lord!"

— Diary, 1289

SECRET 7

Scripture

"As the Father has loved me, so have I loved you; abide in my
love."

— John 15:9

"These things I have spoken to you, that my joy may be in
you, and that your joy may be full."

— John 15:11

"You will seek me and find me; when you seek me with all
your heart, I will be found by you, says the Lord."

— Jeremiah 29:13-14

Catechism

"The life of prayer is the habit of being in the presence of the thrice-holy God and in communion with Him. This communion of life is always possible because, through Baptism, we have already been united with Christ."

— CCC, 2565

"Spiritual progress tends toward ever more intimate union with Christ. This union is called 'mystical' because it participates in the mystery of Christ through the sacraments — 'the holy mysteries' — and, in him, in the mystery of the Holy Trinity. God calls us all to this intimate union with him."

— CCC, 2014

Diary of St. Faustina

"I often feel God's presence after Holy Communion in a special and tangible way. I know God is in my heart. And the fact that I feel Him in my heart does not interfere with my duties. Even when I am dealing with very important matters which require attention, I do not lose the presence of God in my soul, and I am closely united with Him. With Him I go to work, with Him I go for recreation, with Him I suffer, with Him I rejoice; I live in Him and He in me. I am never alone, because He is my constant companion. He is present to me at every moment. Our intimacy is very close, through a union of blood and of life."

— Diary, 318

"After Holy Communion, I felt the beating of the heart of Jesus in my own heart. Although I have been aware, for a long time, that Holy Communion continues in me until the next Communion, today —and throughout the whole day— I am adoring Jesus in my heart. ... A vivid and even physically felt presence of God continues throughout the day and does not in the least interfere with my duties."

— Diary, 1821

"I long without cease to be eternally united with my God; and the better I know Him, the more ardently I desire Him."

— Diary, 1303